101 HILARIOUS CAT JOKES & RIDDLES FOR KIDS

Laugh Out Loud With These Funny Jokes About Cats (WITH 35+ PICTURES)!

© Copyright 2020 by Cesar Dunbar – All rights reserved.

In no way is it legal to reproduce, duplicate, or transmit any part of this document in either electronic means or in printed format. Recording of this publication is strictly prohibited and any storage of this document is not allowed unless with written permission from the publisher.

The information provided herein is stated to be truthful and consistent, in that any liability, in terms of inattention or otherwise, by any usage or abuse of any policies, processes, or directions contained within is the solitary and utter responsibility of the recipient reader. Under no circumstances will any legal responsibility or blame be held against the author for any reparation, damages, or monetary loss due to the information herein, either directly or indirectly.

The information herein is offered for informational purposes solely, and is universal as so. The presentation of the information is without contract or any type of guarantee assurance.

Medical Disclaimer: The jokes contained in this book are not intended as a substitute for consulting with your veterinary physician. All matters regarding your cat's health require medical supervision.

Legal Disclaimer: all illustrations used in this book are designed by Freepik. The photos in the bonus chapter are licensed for commercial use or in the public domain.

Table of Contents

INTRODUCTION 6
101 HILARIOUS CAT JOKES & RIDDLES 11
BONUS JOKES 116
DID YOU LIKE THIS BOOK? 128
OTHER BOOKS BY THIS AUTHOR 131

INTRODUCTION

First joke: *What is every cat's favorite movie?*

Answer: *The Purrrr-minator!*

Thank you for picking up a copy of '*101 Hilarious Cat Jokes For Kids*'.

Let me get straight to the point: If you want to laugh about cats, you don't need this book. **All you need is a cat**!

You know what I'm talking about: it's a lazy Sunday afternoon, you're chilling on the couch, looking at that furry ball of cuteness. And within 30 seconds she's *doing something* – or even just *looking at you in that special way* – and next thing you know you're **rolling on the floor with laughter**!

Did that ever happen to you?

Seriously, if you don't own a cat: if you want cheap entertainment, **get a cat**! It'll be the *best* investment you'll ever make.

But, who knows:

- maybe you feel bad about laughing at your cat all the time
- or perhaps you don't own a cat yet and are in dire need of some meow-tastic comedy
- Or you are simply looking to share some laughs *with* your fuzzy furry friend.

Well, you have come to the right place!

This book is jam-packed with:

- 100+ hilarious cat jokes, and

- 30+ funny illustrations

that will have you *grin*, *LOL*, and *roar with laughter*.

So, I hope you are ready: **let's have a laugh about the world's best pet!**

101 HILARIOUS CAT JOKES & RIDDLES

1.

Q: What do you call a cat that lives in an igloo?

A: An eskimew!

2.

Q: What do you call at cat that goes bowling?

A: An alley cat

3.

A cat went to the post office to send a telegram. He took out a blank form and wrote: "*Meow. Meow. Meow. Meow. Meow. Meow. Meow. Meow. Meow.*"

When he was done, he gave it to the clerk. The clerk looked at the paper and said to the cat: "*There are only 9 words here. We have a special offer: You could send another 'Meow' for the same price.*"

To which the cat replied: "*Sorry, but that wouldn't make any sense at all!*"

4.

Q: What's the difference between a cat and a comma?

A: One has claws at the end of its paws, while the other is a pause at the end of a clause.

5.

Q: What did the alien say to the cat?

A: "Take me to your litter."

6.

Q: What would a cat say if you stepped on its tail?

A: "Me-OW!"

7.

Q: What is a cat's favorite color?

A: Purrrple

8.

Q: What's a cat's favorite dessert?

A: mice cream!

9.

Q: What do you get if you cross a leopard with a watchdog?

A: A terrified postman!

10.

Q: What do you call a pile of kittens?

A: a meowntain

11.

Q: Why don't cats like online shopping?

A: They prefer a cat-alogue.

12.

Q: What did the cat on the smart phone say?

A: Can you hear meow?

13.

Q: Why are cats so good at video games?

A: Because they have nine lives!

14.

Q: Who did cats vote for in November 2016?

A: Hillary Kitten.

15.

Q: Why was the cat sitting on the computer?

A: To keep an eye on the mouse!

16.

Q: What did the cat say when he lost his toys?

A: You got to be kitten me.

17.

Q: What do you get if you cross a tiger with a sheep?

A: A stripey sweater!

18.

Q: What happens when a dog chases a cat into a geyser?

A: It starts raining cats and dogs.

19.

Q: What is a French cat's favorite pudding?

A: Chocolate mousse!

20.

Q: What was the name of the film about a killer lion that swam underwater?

A: 'Claws.'

21.

Q: How do cats get over a fight?

A: They hiss and make up.

22.

Q: What did the cat say to the dog?

A: Check meow-t!

23.

Q: What do you get if you cross a dog and a cheetah?

A: A dog that chases cars – and catches them!

24.

Q: What do you get if you cross a cat with a dark horse?

A: Kitty Perry

25.

Q: What happens when it rains cats and dogs?

A: You can step in a poodle!

26.

Q: What kind of sports car does a cat drive?

A: a Furrari.

27.

One day, a man visited his friend. When he walked into the living room, he found his friend playing chess with his cat.

Astonished, he watched the game for a couple of minutes. "*I can't believe my eyes!*" he exclaimed. "*That is the smartest cat I have ever seen.*"

To which his friend replied: "*Mwoah, he's not that smart. I've beaten him three games out of five.*"

28.

A man in a movie theater notices what looks like a cat sitting next to him. "*Are you a cat?*" asked the man, surprised. "*Yes*", said the cat.

"*What are you doing at the movies?*"

The cat replied, "*Well, I liked the book.*"

29.

Q: What is it called when a cat wins a dog show?

A: A CAT-HAS-TROPHY!

30.

Q: What do you call a cat that gets anything it wants?

A: Purrr-suasive.

31.

Q: What do you call a flying cat?

A: I'm-paws-sible.

32.

Q: What happened when the lion ate the comedian?

A: He felt funny!

33.

Q: What is the cat's favorite TV show?

A: The evening mews!

34.

Q: Why was the cat scared of the tree?

A: Because of its bark.

35.

While mending fences out on the range, a very religious cowboy lost his favorite Bible. He was devastated!

Three weeks later, however, a cat walked up to him, carrying that same Bible in its mouth.

The cowboy was astonished, he couldn't believe it! He took the precious book out of the cat's mouth, thanked him, went on his knees and exclaimed: *"It's a miracle!"*.

To which the cat replied: *"Not really. Your name is written inside the cover."*

36.

A man takes his cat to the vet, because he is cross-eyed.

The vet says: *"Let's have a look"* and picks up the cat to examine his eyes. After looking at his eyes for a while, the vet says: *"I'm going to have to put him down."*

"Wait, what?" the man replies, *"Just because he is cross-eyed?"*

Vet: *"No, because he is really heavy!"*

37.

Q: What do you call a painting of a cat?

A: A paw-trait

38.

Q: What's more amazing than a talking cat?

A: A spelling bee.

39.

Q: Did you hear about the cat that climbed the Himalayas?

A: She was a sher-paw.

40.

Q: Why did the cat wear a dress?

A: She was feline fine.

41.

Q: How does a lion greet the other animals in the field?

A: "Pleased to eat you!"

42.

Q: Why did the cat put the letter "M" into the fridge?

A: Because it turns "ice" into "mice"!

43.

Q: What did the cat say when he lost all his money?

A: I'm paw!

44.

A policeman stops a man in a car with a Puma in the front seat. "*What are you doing with that Puma?*", he asked. "*You should take it to the zoo!*"

The next week, the same policeman sees the same man with the Puma again in the front seat. This time, both are wearing sunglasses.

The policeman pulls the car over. "*I thought you were going to take it to the zoo!*" The man replied, "*I did. We had such a great time we are going to the beach this weekend!*"

45.

Q: What is a cat's favorite chocolate bar?

A: Kit Kat

46.

A cat walks into a job center. "*Wow, a talking cat,*" says the clerk. "*With your talent, I'm sure we can find you a gig in the circus.*" "*The circus?*" says the cat, disappointed: "*What does a circus want with a plumber?*"

47.

A man took his guinea pig to the vet. The doctor shook his head as he looked at the guinea pig.

"*I'm sorry, I'm afraid your guinea pig is dead*" said the vet.

"*Wait, what, how could you be so sure?*" the man replied.

So the vet left the room and come back with a Labrador Retriever. The dog stood up on its hind legs, sniffed the guinea pig and shook its head.

Next, the vet left the room again. This time, he came back with a cat. The cat also sniffed the guinea pig and also shook its head.

The vet said that the guinea pig was 100% dead.

With the man still in shock, the vet handed him the bill.

He looked at the bill, in disbelief: "*$500, why $500?*"

The vet replied "*If you had believed me when I first said it, it would have been $75. But you didn't believe me. So, to confirm the death, you also had a lab report and a cat scan!*"

48.

Q: Why was the cat disqualified from the game?

A: It was a cheetah.

49.

Did you hear about the cat who swallowed a ball of wool?

She had mittens!

50.

Q: What is the cat's favorite magazine?

A: Good Mousekeeping.

51.

Q: How many cats can you put into an empty box?

A: Only one. After that, the box isn't empty.

52.

Q: What is a cat's favorite movie?

A: The Sound of Mewsic.

53.

Q: What do you use to comb a cat?

A: catacomb.

54.

A man drives deep into the woods to get rid of his cat. He lets her out at an abandoned place. After 30 minutes, his wife calls him: "*The cat is back...*"

The man growls: "*Oh man...Ehm, can you put her on please? I got lost and need directions.*"

55.

Two cats are sitting in front of bird's cage and observe a newly arrived green canary. One cat says to the other, "*It really is a strange color for a bird. Maybe he's not ripe yet.*"

56.

A woman sits in a restaurant. All of a sudden, a cat walks in, buys a banana ice cream and leaves.

The woman is astounded: *"Wow, that's so strange!"*.

The restaurant manager: *"Yeah, I agree, up until today she always ordered chocolate ice cream."*

57.

Q: Why was the cat such a good storyteller?

He knew how to paws for dramatic effect.

58.

Q: What do you get if you cross a tiger with a snowman?

A: Frostbite!

59.

Q: Why do cats make terrible dance partners?

A: They've got two left feet!

60.

Q: What is a cat's favorite car?

A: Catillac

61.

Q: What kind of cat eats with their ears?

A: They all do! Who removes their ears before dinner?

62.

Q: Why did the cat sleep under the car?

A: Because he wanted to wake up oily.

63.

Q: Why can't cats work the TV remote when watching Netflix?

A: Because they always hit the 'paws' button!

64.

Q: Why was the cat so small?

A: When it grew up, it only ate condensed milk!

65.

Knock, knock.

Who's there?

Kitten.

Kitten, who?

Quit kitten around and open the door!

66.

Q: How do you make a cat happy?

A: Send it to the Canary Islands!

67.

Two moms discuss how to get their sons to wake up in the morning, to get them to school on time.

"How do you get your sleepy-head son up in the morning?", the first mom asked. The other mom replied: *"I just put the cat on the bed."*

"Huh, how does that help?"

The other mom: *"The dog's already there..."*

68.

Q: Who delivers presents to cats?

A: Santa Claws!

69.

What is the first thing a cat does in the morning?
It wakes up.

What is the second thing it does after waking up?
It goes back to sleep.

70.

3 cats were sitting together on the rug.

The first cat said, "*Meow.*" Next, the second cat said, "*Meow.*" Then, the third cat said, "*Meow, meow.*"

The first cat said, "*Hey, don't change the subject.*"

71.

A mother mouse and a baby mouse are walking along when suddenly a cat attacks them.

The mother mouse shouts "*WOOF!*" and the cat runs away, scared.

"*See?*" the mother mouse says to her baby. "*Now do you see why it's important to learn a foreign language?*"

72.

Did you hear about the cat who joined the Red Cross?

She became a first aid kit!

73.

A young girl felt bad after she accidentally let the neighbor's cat get loose. After 2 weeks, the missing cat seemed to be gone for good.

"*I'm so sorry,*" the girl told the neighbor. "*I'd like to replace it for you.*"

"O.K.," the neighbor said. "*How good are you at catching mice?*"

74.

Q: What do you call a cat that gives up?

A: a quitty!

75.

Q: What do you call a confused cat?

A: Purr-plexed.

76.

A couple were going to see a movie and ordered a taxi. As the couple left the house, their cat ran back in. The husband went back inside, because they didn't want the cat to be shut in the house while they were away. The wife stepped into the taxi.

Because she didn't want the taxi driver to know that the house was empty, she told him that her husband had just gone inside to say goodbye to her mother.

A short while later, her husband also stepped into the cab and said: *"My apologies for taking so long, but that stupid old thing was hiding under the bed. I had to poke her with a broomstick to get her to come out!"*

77.

Q: What do you get when you cross a cat with a parrot?

A: A carrot.

78.

Q: What kind of musician do cats like to be?

A: Purr-cussionists.

79.

Q: How is a cat like a coin?

A: It has a head on one side and tail on the other.

80.

Q: How does a cat sing scales?

A: Do-re-mi-ow!

81.

Q: Why was the cat so crabby?

A: He was in a bad mewd!

82.

Knock, Knock!

Who's there?

Neil!

Neil who?

Neil down and pet the cat before he loses his temper!

83.

Knock, Knock!

Who's there?

Claw.

Claw who?

It's Claw Enforcement. You have the right to remain silent. Anything you say or do may be used against you in a court of meow.

84.

Q: Did you hear about the cat who invented the knock knock joke?

A: She won the no-bell prize!

85.

Q: What award do cat journalists earn?

A: The Purr-litzer prize.

86.

Q: What do cats wear to smell good?

A: Purr-fume.

87.

Q: Why is it so hard for leopards to hide?

A: Because they're always spotted!

88.

Q: How do you know cats are sensitive?

A: They cry over spilt milk.

89.

Q: What state has the most cats?

A: Petsylvania

90.

Q: Where do cats go after their tails fall off?

A: The re-tail store.

91.

Q: What kind of yard work do cats like the most?

A: Meowing the lawn.

92.

Q: Why do cats make the best pets?

A: Because they are purr-fect!

93.

Q: What type of cat has eight legs and loves to swim?

A: An octopuss.

94.

Q: Where did the kittens go for their school field trip?

A: The mewseum.

95.

Q: In what month do cats meow the least?

A: February, it's the shortest month!

96.

A three-legged cat walks into a bar.

He says: *"I'm looking for the man who shot my paw!"*

97.

Q: What should you say to your cat when leave for school?

A: Have a mice day.

98.

Q: Why do Cat Vampires believe everything you tell them?

A: Because they're suckers!

99.

Q: What is a cat's favorite school subject?

A: HISStory.

100.

Two criminals are about to break out of prison. The first one jumps off a wall into a trash container. The guard, alarmed by the noise, shouts "*Who's there?*". The criminal replies, "*MEOOOW!*" The guard is relieved, "*Ah I see, it's just a cat.*"

Then, the second criminal jumps, also making some noise. The guard now gets suspicious and asks, "*Hello, who is there?*" To which the second criminal replies, "*Nobody, it's just the cat again!*"

101.

A cat sits in a bar, sipping a whiskey.

A customer walks up to him and says, "*Wow, it's not often that I see a cat drinking bourbon here!*"

To which the cat replies: *"Yeah, but that's hardly a surprise at these prices."*

BONUS JOKES

These are <u>11 bonus jokes</u> from my popular book *'101 Hilarious Dog Jokes For Kids.*

Enjoy!

***

1.

Q: What do you call a dog magician?

A: A labracadabrador!

2.

Q: What do you call a dog with a surround system?

A: A sub-woofer.

3.

Knock, knock!

Who's there?

Ron.

Ron who?

Ron a little faster, will you? There's a Pitbull after us!

4.

Q: What did the dog say when he sat on sandpaper?

A: Ruff!

5.

Q: What do you get when you cross a race dog with a bumble bee?

A: A Greyhound Buzz

6.

Q: What do you call a large dog that meditates?

A: Aware wolf.

7.

Q: What do you call a frozen dog?

A: A pupsicle.

8.

Q: What do you get when you cross a dog and a calculator?

A: A friend you can count on.

9.

Q: What do you call a cold dog?

A: A Chili Dog

10.

Q: How are a dog and a marine biologist alike?

A: One wags a tail and the other tags a whale.

11.

Q: What do you get if you cross a dog with a frog?

A: A dog that can lick you from the other side of the road!

***

This is the end of this bonus chapter.

Want to continue reading?

Then get your copy of "101 Dog Jokes" at your favorite bookstore!

DID YOU LIKE THIS BOOK?

If you enjoyed this book, I would like to ask you for a favor. Would you be kind enough to share your thoughts and post a review of this book? Just a few sentences would already be really helpful.

Your voice is important for this book to reach as many people as possible.

The more reviews this book gets, the more people will be able to find it and have a good laugh with these funny cat jokes!

***

IF YOU DID NOT LIKE THIS BOOK, THEN PLEASE TELL ME! You can email me at **feedback@semsoli.com**, to share with me what you did not like.

Perhaps I can change it.

A book does not have to be stagnant, in today's world. With feedback from readers like yourself, I can improve the book. So, you can impact the quality of this book, and I welcome your feedback. Help make this book better for everyone! Thank you again for reading this book: I hope you had a good laugh :).

OTHER BOOKS BY THIS AUTHOR